Ripley's
RUGBY RUBBISH

Ripley's
RUGBY RUBBISH
The Essential Ego and Massage Book

ANDY RIPLEY

London
GEORGE ALLEN & UNWIN
Boston   Sydney

Acknowledgements

The author and publishers wish to thank
Colorsport
and
Mike Brett Photography
for their assistance in supplying the many and varied
photographs herein.

George Allen & Unwin (Publishers) Ltd,
40 Museum Street, London WC1A 1LU, UK

George Allen & Unwin (Publishers) Ltd,
Park Lane, Hemel Hempstead, Herts HP2 4TE, UK

Allen & Unwin Inc.,
Fifty Cross Street, Winchester, Mass. 01890, USA

George Allen & Unwin Australia Pty Ltd,
8 Napier Street, North Sydney, NSW 2060, Australia

First published 1985

ISBN 004 796105 8

Set in 11 on 13 point Clear Face Regular and printed in Great Britain by
William Clowes Ltd., Beccles, Suffolk

Foreword

In the unlikely event that this load of junk
generates a few spondulicks, net of costs and
the publishers' rapacious overheads, all net
monies will be given to "The National Society
for Prevention of Cruelty to Children"
(Honest).

This is because, not only do I want to be
President of the Rugby Football Union in 1994
but also because I am a truly wonderful person
and books like this don't make much money.

Andy Ripley
Hoping for an MBE
London, 1985

This book is dedicated to:-

The Germanic Peoples

My Mum

Lord Carrington

People who live in Glass Houses

Toby Allchurch

Marcus Allen

Peter York

Jean Jacques Cousteau

Sir Terence Beckett

Jill Tweedie

Some French Canadians

Bob Penberthy

The Bangkok Book Index

Steve Bell

Joanna Parkinson

H.M. Sultan Qaboos

William Caxton's Sister

Albert Fraser

and

Sargie Boy

Editorial Advice

The publisher of this fab book told me in order for
us to go for market share and to be cost effective
I had to mention four things:

1. *Superstars*

2. *Superstars*

3. *Superstars*

4. *Superstars*

Ancillary to these four sections I could mention in
passing three other subjects:

5. Dirty sex on rugby tours with names, dates
and places.

6. Transfer of money in brown envelopes with
names, dates and places.

7. *Superstars*

Finally, if I was getting really desperate I could
write about:

8. *Superstars*

George Allen & Unwin

40 Museum Street, London WC1A 1LU. England. Tel: 01 405 8577

Andy Ripley
Sometime Moneylender   31st August 1984
United Bank of Kuwait
3 Lombard Street
London EC3V 9DT

Dear Andy

ANDY RIPLEY'S RUBBISH

First, nought out of ten for the title.

Secondly, I would be prepared to offer you three thousand
spondulicks for Rubbish. Please let me know which Geneva
account I should pay it into.

Thirdly, we shall need a book club deal to shore-up the risk.

Fourthly, I have completed the editing and await your
response.

Fifthly:

Yours sincerely

DEREK WYATT
Editor

Telex: 826261 Answer Code: GAU G Cable: Deucalion London WC1 Giro Number: 3751252. Registration: London 13733¹
George Allen & Unwin (Publishers) Ltd. Registered Head Office: 40 Museum Street, London WC1A 1LU.

WHERE THE HEART IS

4th September 1984

George Allen & Unwin
40 Museum Street
London WC1A 1LU

<u>A CONTRACT</u>

Dear Derek,

You and your company can have this heap of self indulgence
to do with as you wish, provided:

(1) If and when it gets close to its final state, I can
file it in the waste paper basket if it's too crumby to
live.

(2) You give the best possible deal on fees and royalties
since any money is going to the NSPCC and you print
your response next to this letter
so the world and his brother can see what George Allen
& Unwin consider a good deal to be.

(3) You buy each of the two girls who typed this a big
clock.

(4) You undertake to make sure that this book is never used
for exam purposes.

Stay Fab.

George Allen & Unwin 40 Museum Street, London WC1A 1LU. England. Tel: 01 405 8577

5th September 1984

Andy Ripley
Occasional Wit
United Bank of Kuwait
3 Lombard Street
London   EC3V 9DT

Dear Andy,

In response to your letter of 4th September 1984:

1. I quite like John Craven.

2. I promise to do just that.

3. I have contacted Westminster.

4. I have written to Sir Keith Joseph.

Best wishes.

Yours sincerely,

Derek Wyatt
EDITOR

Telex: 826261 Answer Code: GAU G Cable: Deucalion London WC1 Giro Number: 3751252. Registration: London 137338.

George Allen & Unwin (Publishers) Ltd. Registered Head Office: 40 Museum Street, London WC1A 1LU.

ON CHOOSING A TITLE

Someone told me that someone had told them that they'd heard from a bloke in a McDonalds who'd seen Alan Coren on a TV programme, who'd reportedly said that, 'titles sell books' and particularly if the title mentions:

GARDENING
ANIMALS
COOKERY
SEX
and
THE WAR

So really every book which is looking to the bottom line, could be entitled:

"SELF-FLAGELLATION FOR HUNGRY HAMSTERS ON A COUNCIL ALLOTMENT IN A POST NUCLEAR AGE"

Now this could be thought of as being a bit forced. So I came up with what I thought was a real winner:

"HITLER'S BOOK OF CATS"

For some reason the publishers, who'd fought through two World Wars, blah blah, didn't like it, so they suggested the very subtle title:

"RUCK OFF RIPLEY"

Fucking fantastic, I thought.

So we worked our way through:

"36 HANDY RECIPES FOR HOMOSEXUAL POLAR BEARS"

"A GUIDE TO FAST FOOD CHAIN STORES IN EAST GERMANY"

"WASTED SPACE, BLAH BLAH BLAH"

to eventually

"ANDY RIPLEY'S RUBBISH? RUGBY ISN'T"

Life's a compromise. John.

RUGBY PLAYERS EASY TO WRITE RUGBY BOOK GUIDE

At home we were
1. so poor, we played football.
2. pretty average.
3. so rich, I've been privileged all my life.

I am looking forward to
1. suing the Daily Telegraph.
2. heavy royalties man.
3. being a sports commentator.

I first played rugby
1. in the back field with a dead rat for a ball, little did I know then, etc. etc.
2. for the school 6th XV, little did I know then, etc. etc.
3. for England.

I owe it all to
1. my coach at school.
2. Budge Rogers
3. Sanatogen

I remember my first international because
1. it was my last
2. the thrill of Pulling On the jersey, etc. etc.

One of the greatest moments of my career was
1. beating the All Blacks, Lions, Springboks, Wales, etc.
2. being asked to speak at DISS, R.F.C. annual dinner (twice)
3. seeing John Reason and Terry O'Connor fighting at East London Airport.

One of the worst aspects of my rugby career was
1. being dropped
2. going to New Zealand instead of the Bahamas.
3. my injury. blah, blah, blah

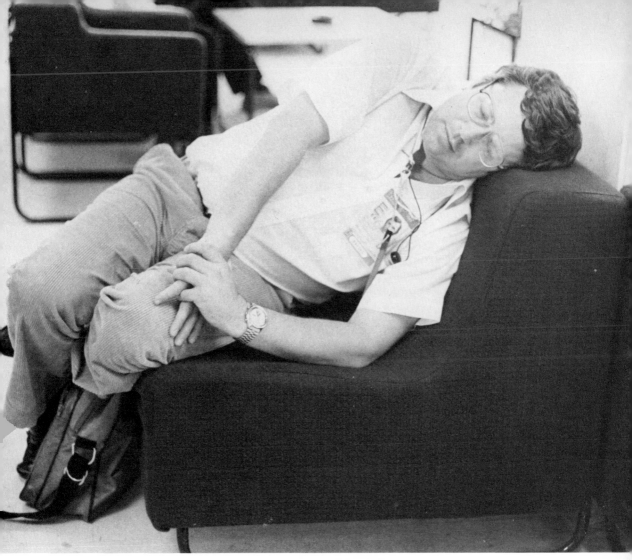

SOME DAY MY PRINCE WILL COME

Barry Newcombe, dynamic rugby correspondent of the Sunday Express, puts in another hard day's graft.

My views on South Africa are
1. pretty average.
2. in the formative stage.
3. amazingly boring.
4. where's South Africa?

Note: You'll need to pad it out a bit — David Norrie once of the News of the World needs the work and is very good at this and you'll need a few photographs (holiday snap standard will do). Then sit back and wait for the £360 of royalties to just roll on in.

Of the flower of International
British manhood, sacrificed in the
cause of a Victorian Sporting
anachronism:

Ken Goodall

W. B. Beaumont

Barry John

Gareth Edwards

'Mighty Mouse' McLaughlan

David Duckham

Fran Cotton

Micky Burton

Tom David

David Watkins

Keith Fielding

Mike Lampowski

Bob Mordell

Gordon Brown

etc.

Adrian Alexander

etc.

LEST WE FORGET

HOW TO BECOME AN ENGLAND RUGBY FORWARD

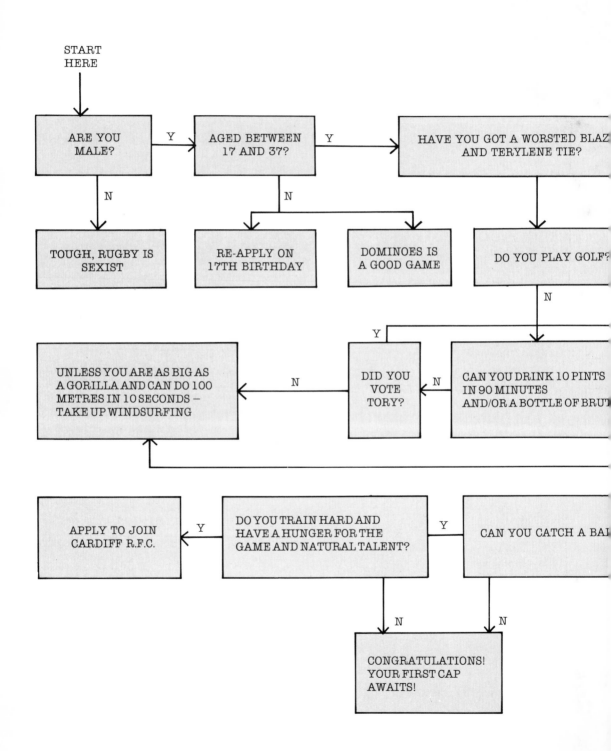

START
HERE

ARE YOU MALE? —Y→ AGED BETWEEN 17 AND 37? —Y→ HAVE YOU GOT A WORSTED BLAZ[ER] AND TERYLENE TIE?

N↓ (ARE YOU MALE?)

N↓ (AGED BETWEEN 17 AND 37?)

TOUGH, RUGBY IS SEXIST

RE-APPLY ON 17TH BIRTHDAY

DOMINOES IS A GOOD GAME

DO YOU PLAY GOLF?

N↓

UNLESS YOU ARE AS BIG AS A GORILLA AND CAN DO 100 METRES IN 10 SECONDS – TAKE UP WINDSURFING

←N— DID YOU VOTE TORY? —N← CAN YOU DRINK 10 PINTS IN 90 MINUTES AND/OR A BOTTLE OF BRUT[?]

Y (to DID YOU VOTE TORY?)

APPLY TO JOIN CARDIFF R.F.C. ←Y— DO YOU TRAIN HARD AND HAVE A HUNGER FOR THE GAME AND NATURAL TALENT? —Y→ CAN YOU CATCH A BAL[L]

N↓ (DO YOU TRAIN HARD...)

N↓ (CAN YOU CATCH A BALL)

CONGRATULATIONS! YOUR FIRST CAP AWAITS!

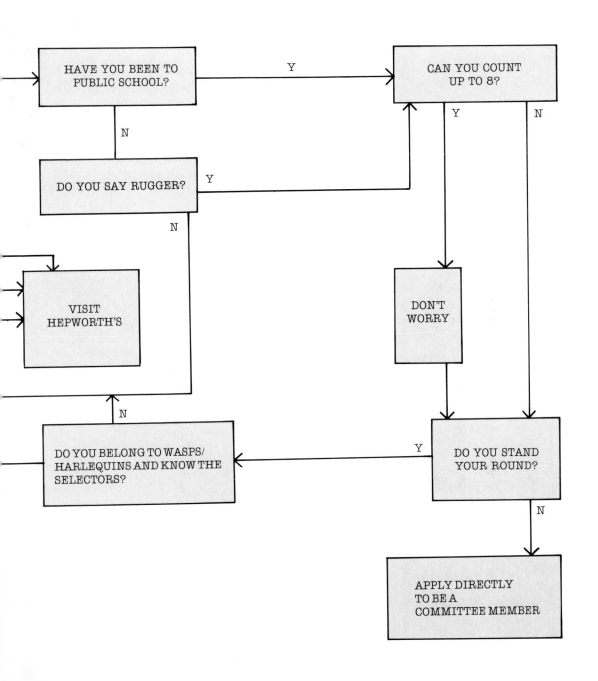

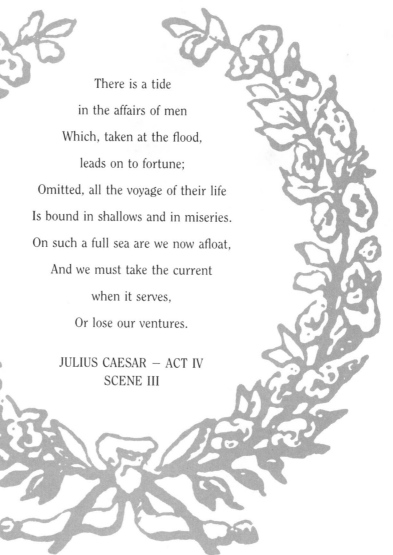

There is a tide

in the affairs of men

Which, taken at the flood,

leads on to fortune;

Omitted, all the voyage of their life

Is bound in shallows and in miseries.

On such a full sea are we now afloat,

And we must take the current

when it serves,

Or lose our ventures.

JULIUS CAESAR – ACT IV
SCENE III

It should have been alright
I can't understand it.

As soon as we got to the ground I got out of the coach backwards and put my left foot on the pavement before my right.

No-one saw me do it.

And I was wearing my lucky red striped shirt with the short sleeves.

I do know that the team bus went under the bridge just after the train had passed but surely two magpies is got to be worth something.

I'd had a cup of tea and stirred the spoon thirteen times anti-clockwise, then put the sugar in and stirred it clockwise eight times.

I'd done everything I should have done.

You can keep all that third light, walking under ladders, opening umbrellas, not picking up fallen knives, spilt salt over the shoulder, green being unlucky, etc., its kids' stuff.

However I had hopped the length of the pitch on my right foot, touched the far posts, then hopped back on my left, remembering to do a 180° turn on each 22 and the half way line. Twice.

No-one saw me.

I didn't start changing until everyone else was changed and then I started.

Kit out of the bag.

Left shoe off, left sock off.

Trousers off.

Shirt off.

Jersey on, saying, "plus two".

$8 + 2$ make 10, divided by 2 makes 5.

Lucky 5. Oh lucky 5.

Underpants off, blue trunks with the red stripe on.

Right shoe off.

Right sock off.

Shorts on.

Left sock on.

Right sock on.

Right boot on.

Left boot on.

Musn't make a mistake. I can remember when we got smacked out of sight when once I'd put the left boot on first.

Team warm up.

1, 2, 3, 4, 5, 6, 7, 8, 9, 10 and all that rubbish.

Last one out of the dressing room; although that Gavin always tries to take my position.

O.K.

I'd done everything just right.

So how is it we're on the wrong end of a right good hiding and I'm playing like a drain.

Oh No! Of course, I forgot my lucky walnut.

I don't believe in God or the minimum
lending rate

I believe in Rugby
because I like good times
and Rugby will marry me

    and give me a good time
    and give me happiness
    and play me around
    and plague me
    and break my heart
    and leave me as I grow older

And then after the good times
there'll be years left for the rest
God and steady won't there
or did Jim Morrison say it first

Spot the Brain Surgeon

```
LIFE IS BRILL N' FAB
LIFE IS BRILL N' FAB
LIFE IS BRILL N' FAB
LIFE IS BRILL N' FAB
LIFE IS BRILL N' FAB
LIFE IS BRILL N' FAB
LIFE IS BRILL N' FAB
LIFE IS BRILL N' FAB
LIFE IS BRILL N' FAB
LIFE IS BRILL N' FAB
LIFE IS BRILL N' FAB
LIFE IS BRILL N' FAB
LIFE IS BRILL N' FAB
LIFE IS BRILL N' FAB
LIFE IS BRILL N' FAB
LIFE IS BRILL N' FAB
LIFE IS BRILL N' FAB
LIFE IS BRILL N' FAB
LIFE IS BRILL N' FAB
LIFE IS BRILL N' FAB
LIFE IS BRILL N' FAB
LIFE IS BRILL N' FAB
LIFE IS BRILL N' FAB
LIFE IS BRILL N' FAB
LIFE IS BRILL N' FAB
LIFE IS BRILL N' FAB
LIFE IS BRILL N' FAB
LIFE IS BRILL N' FAB
LIFE IS BRILL N' FAB
LIFE IS BRILL N' FAB
LIFE IS BRILL N' FAB
LIFE IS BRILL N' FAB
LIFE IS BRILL N' FAB
LIFE IS BRILL N' FAB
LIFE IS BRILL N' FAB
LIFE IS BRILL N' FAB
LIFE IS BRILL N' FAB
LIFE IS BRILL N' FAB
LIFE IS BRILL N' FAB
LIFE IS BRILL N' FAB
LIFE IS BRILL N' FAB
LIFE IS BRILL N' FAB
LIFE IS BRILL N' FAB
LIFE IS BRILL N' FAB
LIFE IS BRILL N' FAB
LIFE IS BRILL N' FAB
LIFE IS BRILL N' FAB
LIFE IS BRILL N' FAB
Life is Fab n' brill
LIFE IS BRILL N' FAB
LIFE IS BRILL N' FAB
LIFE IS BRILL N' FAB
LIFE IS BRILL N' FAB
LIFE IS BRILL N' FAB
LIFE IS BRILL N' FAB
LIFE IS BRILL N' FAB
LIFE IS BRILL N' FAB
LIFE IS BRILL N' FAB
LIFE IS BRILL N' FAB
LIFE IS BRILL N' FAB
LIFE IS BRILL N' FAB
LIFE IS BRILL N' FAB
```

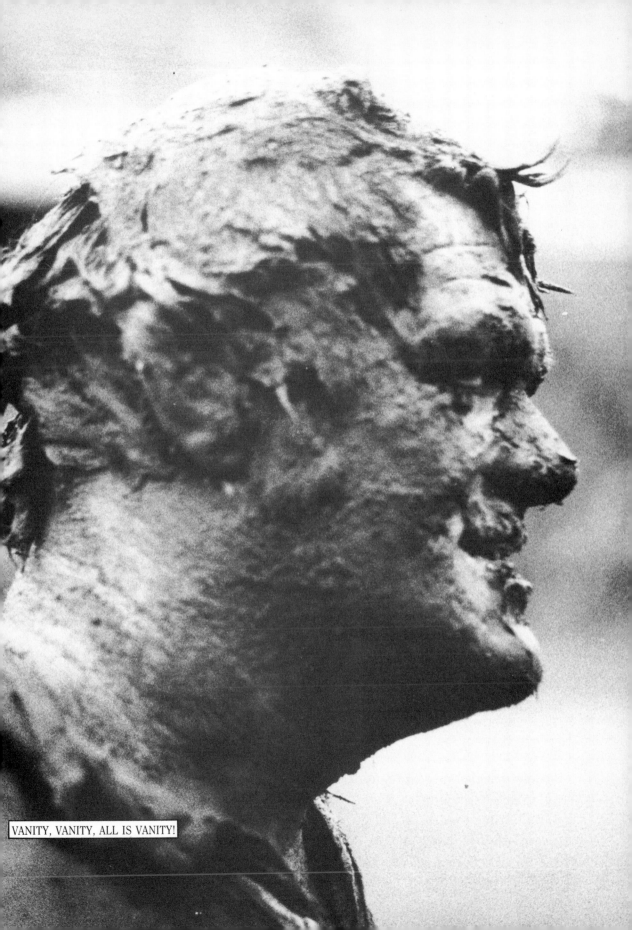

VANITY, VANITY, ALL IS VANITY!

Rugby is something you have to do on a wet cold Thursday afternoon in Bristol when you're 12

Rugby is standing under the posts at Kingsholm twelve minutes into the first half and seeing the ball curl between the post to make the score 0−18

Rugby is appealing to the referee because at 36 that's all you can do

Rugby is changing in an old shed in Holt in 1967 and not speaking at their dinner in 1983

Rugby is a way of getting lucky and giving you a stage, however limited to play a part, however limiting

Rugby is Jan Webster and John Watkins and Chris Ralston

Rugby is Keith Murdoch

Rugby is cutting your head open in a pool B match in the French Divisional Championship in Rouen in 1975

Rugby is not getting picked for the Lions' Test team in 1974. England in 1976, Middlesex in 1983 and Rosslyn Park 1st XV in 1985

Rugby is all this and so much more.

Rugby is beating the All Blacks in New Zealand, The Springboks in Johannesburg and Lowestoft and Yarmouth at Fifer's Lane.

Rugby is breaking your knee cap

Rugby is an introduction for a product of the 1947 Bevan Government welfare and educational schemes to the United Nations' Blacklist

Rugby is a way of making your Mum happy

Rugby is Micky Burton sitting at the back of a bus in Fiji, hotel foyer in Sydney, the Star and Garter in Richmond, telling the same story with everyone still listening

Rugby is Lionel Weston leaving the pitch one cold Saturday in October and never playing again

Rugby is sometimes hijacked by the selectors and the committee but can never be taken away from Steve Smith

Rugby is is two parrots over half a moon

Rugby is retiring after training one Thursday evening in September, using the excuse its 11.30p.m., you've missed your connections and are stuck on East Croydon Station and do you really need it.

Rugby is being phoned up on Friday morning being mildly flattered and coming out of retirement

Rugby sometimes makes you act like an old tart, not that there's anything wrong with old tarts

Rugby is standing around at St. Mary's College in Twickenham with the five other substitutes being used occasionally as a prop or as a marker in the line out

Rugby is being club captain and feeling a responsibility that Nick Watkins' BXV has a ball to play with and a pitch to play on

Rugby is realising that Nick Watkins' BXV can organise themselves, and in any case seem to be enjoying themselves more than you are

Rugby is still beating the Springboks in Johannesburg in 1972 and Sam Doble kicking 6 penalty goals out of 6 from your own half in training and everyone feeling referred pride

Rugby is being the youngest player in the dressing room one day and suddenly being almost the oldest

Rugby is seeing young talented players with the world at their feet, get injured and then not seeing them again

Rugby is knowing it was on

Rugby is Dai Morris

Rugby is realising there are far better ways to spend your time but at 5 to 3 on a Saturday afternoon you'd have a hard job convincing me

Rugby is picking up the paper and seeing Tom David is still knocking 'em down somewhere in some muddy field

Rugby is in Cardiff on a Saturday night after a Barbarians' game, discos, casinos and seeing Donald McDonald with a quarter full bottle of whisky at 5 in the morning in a cafe, well into self destruction

Rugby is hearing that Donald McDonald has got married to a very nice American girl

Rugby is holding the ball in two hands from the base of the scrum and running at the fly half as fast as you can and hitting him

Rugby is feeling strong and oblivious to your own mortality

Rugby is all this also much more

Rugby is being kicked in the head by Micky Fry because you're in a different coloured shirt

Rugby is not kneeing Micky Fry in the face when the opportunity presents itself not because you're a wonderful person, but probably because you're a coward

Rugby is liking Micky Fry in any set of circumstances

Rugby is standing under the posts in Murrayfield in February 1974 and seeing Andy Irvine turn imminent victory into forever 1974 England defeat

Rugby is losing a tooth at Goldington Road and 6 years later have Earl Kirton do you a bridge at a special price

Rugby is realizing you're getting old when you think maybe, just maybe, you should have held on to some of the trappings and dross that came when the jewel momentarily glittered in the sunshine

Rugby is realising as Willie John said "You're as good as your last game and the next game is the important one"

Rugby is realising for Willie John that great and loved captains don't necessarily make great and loved managers

Rugby is one of the few exports that Britain has given to Ireland that is of some value and Dublin is a great place

Rugby is picking the ball from the back of the scrum in 1974 and scoring a try against Wales at Twickenham and realising that "I sort of hit it and it was in the back of the net, Brian" is fairly appropriate

Rugby is players court in Auckland where Jeremy, Paul, Aubrey, George Janim was fined for having too many silly names

Rugby is wet unwashed kit on a Saturday slowly moulding since training on Thursday

The following day, we danced
our way to a resounding victory 59—13

MY LIST OF FAVOURITE BOB'S

Bob Anderson — The only man on whom I perpetrated a mean and nasty act.

Bob Hesford — Son of a family, more famous in sporting circles than the Osmonds are to the Mormon Church.

Bob Weighill — Whose finger is nearer the pulse than most people imagine.

Bob Willis — 'Cos he's fab.

THAT FLANKER SURE GETS AROUND

Rugby Football

    is expanding

        geometrically

           At a rate

                A

                    AR

                    AR^2

                    AR^3

                        Where R is less than one and constant.

But the Rugby Football Union still hasn't got enough balls.

RUGBY AND POLITICS (YAWN)

STONE AGE (2,000 B.C. to 1969)

This was the age of faith. A denial of scientific reasoning and Carwyn James coaching methods. Promising an after life and election to the Welsh Rugby Union Committee (South East Branch) after being dropped from the Welsh International Squad provided you had held a committed and unquestioning belief.

The age was characterized by myths, ceremonies, rites, ritual slaughter, heretics faith and more ceremonies.

The reaction to the established order was based largely on the Greek XV (circa 1500 B.C.) founded on a criticism of faith by objective scientific realism. The leading proponents being Damocritus, Heraclitus (the father of Dialectics) Aristotle and John Dawes.

THE RENAISSANCE (1969 – 1974)

This saw the counter attack of reason and science against dogma, tyranny and fanaticism.

Machiavelli by suggesting that the church had appropriated God for its own end, generated an era of freedom of thought to seek the truth independently of stone age constraints. Luther, Mike Gibson, Erasmus, Gareth Edwards, Descartes, Spinoza and Bobby Windsor saw the emergence of the metaphysical and mechanistic materialist concepts based on the use of reason.

This gave rise to the conflict do we run it in the backs (circa Lions 1971) or do we play to the forwards (circa Lions 1974).

However, apart from the 1971 Lions outbreak, France was the real home of reason over religion, and was characterized by Voltaire, Rousseau, Jo Maso, Danton, Guy and Andre Boniface and Robespierre.

Hume and Willie John McBride, expound the cause of agnostic philosophy and the power of the front five suggesting nothing is certain.

Locke and Micky Burton were/are both definitive materialist atheists, opposing the devine right of kings, the Rugby Football Union Committee and the infallibility of religion.

HELLO BOYS

A PERIOD OF TURMOIL (1975–1985)

In the stone age we had experienced idealism which had assumed the existence of super natural and demonic forces (the Welsh R.F.U.). Materialism had considered nothing beyond natural things (the 1949 Irish Grand Slam Side). However the scientific discoveries of the 18th century developed a mechanistic approach (John Burgess) which in turn generated a metaphysical reaction (Sandy Carmichael).

However superimposed on these myriad of thoughts, ideas and reasoning, running right back to Heroclitus in the stone age, the father of the art of argument (along with Brian Price) was the belief in dialectics.

Hegel was a dialectical idealist while his leading edge pupil Feuerbach was more of a metaphysical materialist. Much like Des Seabrook's relationship with Frannie Cotton in the Lancashire County side in 1980.

However it wasn't until the end of this period that Marx developed his changing, evolving form of reason based on science, usually referred to as dialectical materialism. This evolution of thought owes much to the boredom of sitting through the 5 nations Home Championship and watching the talented individuals involved in an 80 minutes goal-kicking contest.

(Contd A.D. 2125)

NO, IT WOULD NOT

Wouldn't it be just terrific to be an All Black and then to run the length of the field and score the winning try in the far right hand corner, they said.

Wouldn't it be just terrific to be the length of the field and pole vault to the corner, he said.

Wouldn't it be just terrific to run the length of the field and score with an All Black in the far right hand corner, she said.

Wouldn't it be just terrific to be an all black All Black, said the Nigerian ambassador, pole vaulting to the corner of the field.

A Nice Day in the Park

A SATIRICAL HYPERBOLE

In 1971 a Vietnamese Prince, fleeing Vietnam's
Tay Son rebels sought refuge with John Richardson
in Aberavon Rugby Football Club.
Unfortunately, John Richardson was becoming somewhat
eccentric and had his guest disembowelled
in search of a diamond which a dream had instructed
him was in his stomach — it was not.

Rugby Anarchists and Syndicalists Ethic

Proundhon, who developed the theory Rugby is Theft, was much influenced by Louis Blanc, who hated all organised sport but left the England Rugby selectors with their 'selection maxim' — 'Reject each according to his ability, select each according to my needs'.

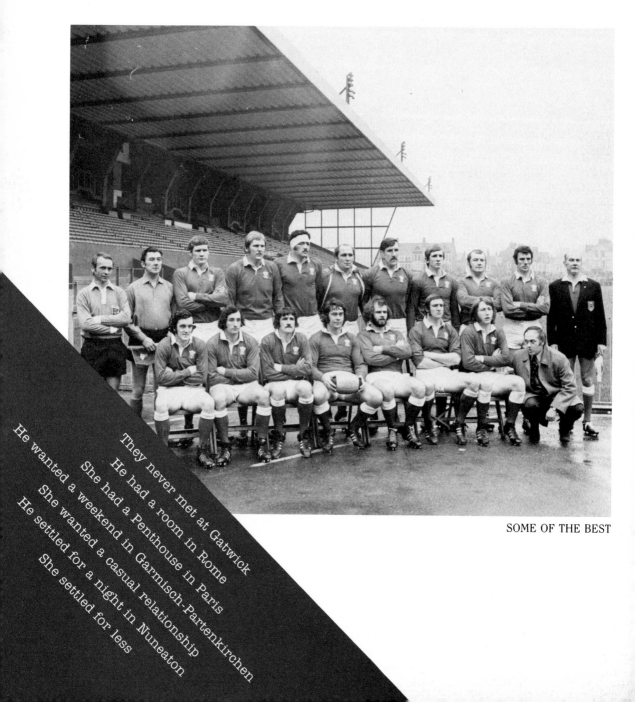

SOME OF THE BEST

They never met at Gatwick
He had a room in Rome
She had a Penthouse in Paris
He wanted a weekend in Garmisch-Partenkirchen
She wanted a casual relationship
He settled for a night in Nuneaton
She settled for less

Marxist-Leninist Rugby Players Creed

Private ownership of the means of production and the ball is the maximum form of alienation. Alienation not only degrades a player but it depersonalises him, so that he is a mere appendage of flesh on a machine of iron. Although labour may earn the worker a wage it deprives him of something which goes into the committee's pockets. Losing a ball in loose play and the free market economy result in alienation, deprivation and depersonalisation for the average member of the West Hartlepool 1st XV.

They met at Gatwick
He hadn't a room in Rome
She hadn't a Penthouse in Paris
He wanted a casual relationship
She wanted a casual relationship
They settled for a casual relationship

Rugby Capitalist's Rhetoric

The objective of most of the East Grinstead Second XV is 'To Possess Possessions in a Free Market Economy' and a good ball in a loose ruck situation. The capitalist Rugby player aspires to own property and the ball. The purpose of life is to possess more but the more he gets the less he keeps of himself. The misery of the masses stems from the possession of the ball by the opposing side and the luxury of the full back.

Utopian Rugby Socialists Dogma

There is no scientific basis for this type of Rugby Player, who is often a prop and who does not acknowledge the class struggle but is more interested in favourite techniques of head butting. They usually believe that religious morality suffices to eliminate social inequalities. This was the view put forward by the New Zealand prop John Ashbourne to J. P. R. Williams one evening at the Brewery Field in Bridgend in 1981.

They met in a room in Rome.
He had had a casual relationship in Paris.
She had never had a caring relationship anywhere.
She wanted a Penthouse in Rome.
She still wanted a Penthouse in Rome.
He went to Gatwick.

OF COURSE IT'S ONLY A
SLIGHT GRAZE JOHN

THE CHARACTERISTICS OF VARIOUS RUGBY TOURS

International Teams	**Club Sides**
Penicillin	Penicillin
5 Star Hotels — buy your own wine	Getting hosted
Rugby Pitches	Meet for training outside McDonalds
Buses	Cars, sometimes coaches
Aeroplanes	Charter flights
After Match Functions	Space Invaders
Pre Match Functions	Nurses' Disco
Afternoon Functions	Getting Drunk
Evening Functions	Losing at Cards
Trying to find someone to sleep with	
Making Friends	Swapping addresses

SOUVENIRS OF THE RED LIGHT DISTRICT

BARBARIAN 7 A SIDE WINNERS OF 1981 HONG KONG 7'S IN THEIR TOUR KIT

Seeing Places but Seeing Nowhere	Trying to find someone to sleep with
Meeting people but really Meeting No-one	
No bills	Costs about £150 and spending money
A few quid a day	
Someone makes a million	Sunshine
Winning games makes life easy	
If it works it's us, Just us – Lions '74	If it works at home, it works away
If it doesn't it's little Groups – England '75	
More buses.	More buses.
Flattered by attention	Flattered by friendship
Did you hear what happened ...	Did you hear what happened to...
Peter Pan	Adolescent
Cotton Wool	Hair Shirt
Up Market Package Tours	Skint

Jeremy Saywell and Friends Big Gig Timetable

VESPERS TERM
Commences 13.1.84

Grace by the Rev. A. Pinfold

School dinners
Boys are reminded not to vomit during the meal

Period 1   History "The Queen"

Period 2   Careers Advice – A. Ripley (R.A.M.C.)

Period 3   Political Science – C. Welland (K.A.N.T.)

Period 4   School Jumble Sale – contact P. Wheeler
            (D.I.P., E.D.)

Period 5   The English Language – Prof. M. Burton

Home Time

The Tuck Shop will be open until 5.30 p.m. No boys can exceed their weekly pocket money allowance unless I have received a note from Matron. *No Excess Tuck.* Pupils are reminded that no wheel-chairs or bicycles are allowed in the Dining Room unless authorised by Matron. Boys caught buggering the Bursar, unless authorised by Matron, will be expelled.

HEADMASTER

Maybe, just maybe, it's not the colour that matters

Write say eight hundred words on some aspect of New Zealand Rugby or any experiences you've had over there while you've been playing Rugby, said the lumpy but lovable Micky Burton.

Well I've always been a soft touch and have never been able to refuse a request from a voice from KINGSHOLM, particularly Micky Burton, who I'm told lists among his cultural interests Millwall, Worthington E, Fish and Chips and watching Crossroads on his unlicensed T.V.

But the big problem, Micky, is that what seemed hilarious/pretty nasty/very dirty in the early hours of a Sunday morning/Tuesday afternoon in some lay-by/hotel just outside AUCKLAND/WANGANUI loses a lot of its appeal when written down in some brightly lit office in London at 11 o'clock in the morning, and in re-reading could definitely win a prize for the most mind bogglingly boring story since the report written by some Fleet Street cub hackette about the most recent meeting of the English Rugby Football Union Committee in full swinging session. ZZZZZZZZZZZZZZZZZZ.................

Anyway New Zealand. New Zealand is long and thin rather like a picturesque Coventry, without the houses, but better looking. It's said to be sexier than Anna Ford and even more exciting than washing the car on a Sunday morning, but that's only a rumour which is very different from the confirmed truth which is that all New Zealanders are over six feet eight inches tall and have good teeth. There are also lots of sheep, which for the most part are fairly butch and not very friendly — still as most of them eventually get eaten that's not too surprising.

Although not quite so evident, but in the same way that most Welshmen over 25 and all Welshmen over 35 are schoolboy internationals, most New Zealanders (especially the males) over 40 have played Rugby for New Zealand, or at least their brother has. This is in fact not a distortion but the 100% truth because another interesting fact about New Zealand is that only

PUBLICITY SEEKER — MOI!

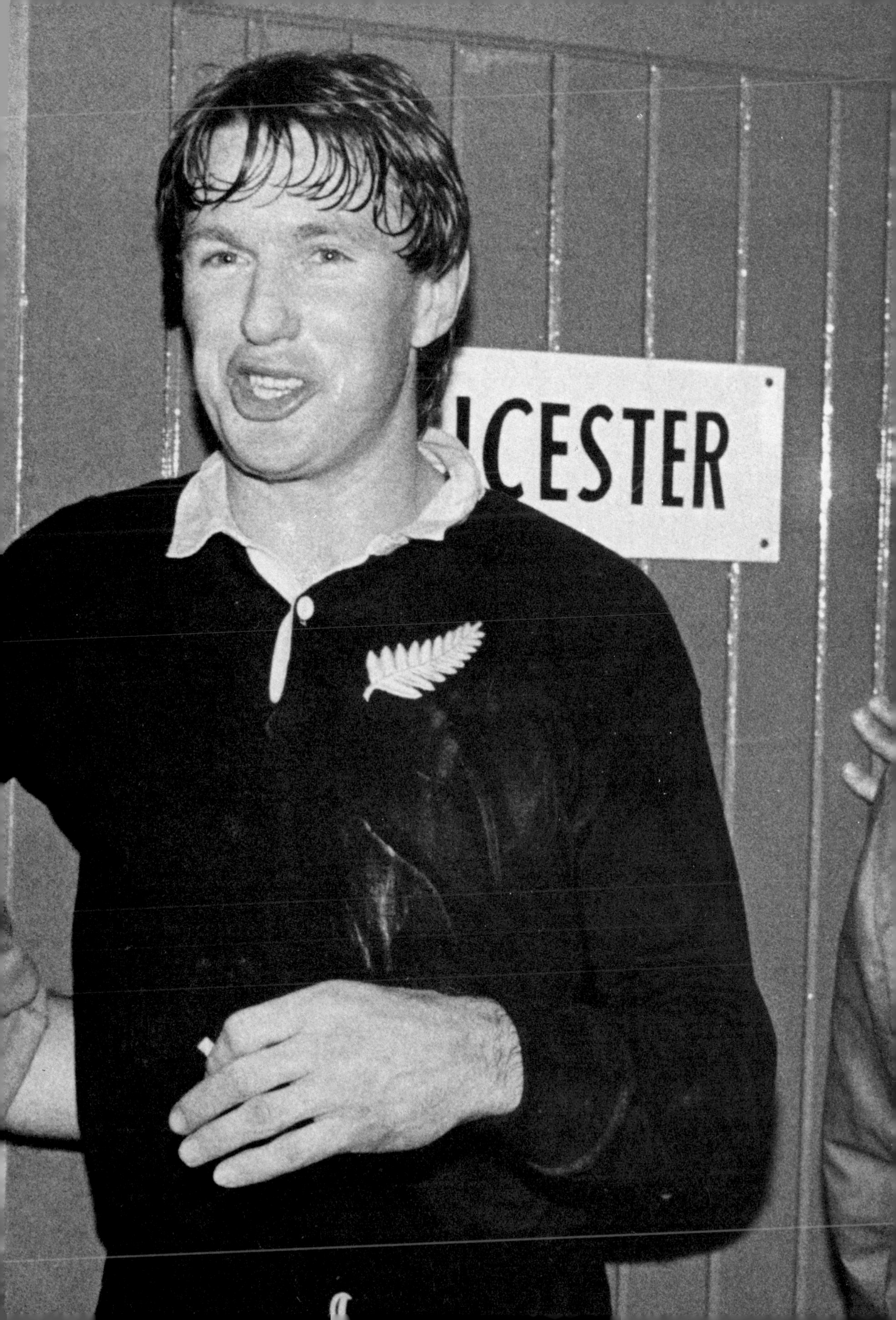
ICESTER

about 50 people live there, so it's always very surprising that they've managed to belt the living daylights out of most teams from the British Isles and Ireland, which as every schoolboy knows has an aggregate but culturally different population of nine hundred million — give or take a few thousand.

Of the 50 people that live in New Zealand and eat sheep about five of them claim to be Originals and they spend all their time, rolling their eyeballs, playing the guitar, sort of dancing, weight lifting, eating hamburgers and generally being fast. The other 45 spend most of their time chasing and eating sheep or sitting in cars listening to the radio.

The current All Black team which is about half the population of New Zealand is an interesting collection of dancers, weight lifters and raw meat eaters. They are, however, all good guys. I know this, because the other half of the population of New Zealand, who are currently driving Volkswagen microbuses around Europe, were at Heathrow when the All Blacks arrived and were heard to shout things as the Air New Zealand DC touched down, like "Hey, here come the good guys."

So, as one of yesterday's men, well OK last month's, who frowns on Sniffin' Glue, might I say to the good guys from New Zealand a big gud-day and welcome.

Because, with the mellowness that comes with age, and now when even the other side of the hill begins to run out, it seems to me that it matters less and less what country you come from or what colour you wear, but what does matter is the friendships you make and the good times behind and ahead.

So my advice, for what it's worth, to the All Blacks, the guys lucky enough to be playing aginst them, the referees, the fab people shouting for them, and the bad guys shouting aginst them and anyone else who has anything else remotely to do with the All Blacks Tour of 1978/79, is enjoy yourselves.

Long may we all keep on trucking, whatever that means. — Rock On.

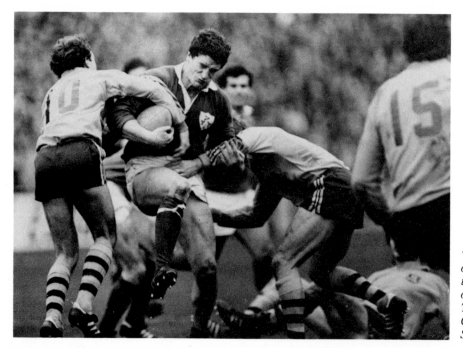

"One of the charms of Rugby Union is the infinite variety of possible tactics"
The Oxford Companion to Sports and Games

ALL I KNOW ABOUT:

SOUTH AFRICA

If you are an average black in South Africa called Wellington by the whites and Jabulani by your Mum you are probably materially better off than the average Jabulani in any other African country.

However, you are not allowed to have dignity. You may actually earn enough to buy a Datsun 180Y but you are restricted where you can go or who you can go with and when and you don't get any say in changing things.

Your average Afrikaaner called Piet has a parent/child relationship with Wellington. Piet usually neither abuses but cannot accept Jabulani as an equal and probably never will. Though Piet, after a fashion, looks after Wellington. Piet is hardworking, puritanical, straight forward and admirable in many ways, although operates from the viewpoint that in his country white is superior to black. English speaking whites called Brian, over tip, over compensate and write letters to the Rand Daily Mail about how shocking everything is. Some new emigrant Brians abuse their position.

What happens to Jabulani, Piet and Brian(s) in a society which is stable and slowly changing but is fundamentally unjust will probably be not much, since as the world polarises, Western Governments need pals and will on one side support trade and diplomatic relations and depending on the flavour of the Western Government, will, shock, horror, have a cheap cost effective cosmetic policy of not playing games with them. That should keep the Nigerian Government happy, as they relocate 2 million Ghanaian people at the point of a gun. Of course Jabulani may decide to change things himself, and who'd blame him. Piet won't like it.

Oh yes, I never bought my own ticket to South Africa, and someone else has always paid the bill and it's always been my good fortune to have been flattered and privileged, and to be shown great hospitality, so maybe I know nothing.

Anyway.

A Review of John Hopkins book on The Lions in S. Africa 1980

If you would have liked to have gone, but didn't actually go, to a comprehensive school, or maybe, just maybe, you spent some time at one of the new universities in the 1980's and have more than just a fleeting interest in Rugby and your friends call you a Gucci Socialist, then relax kid because John Hopkins has written a book just for you. It's a chronological account of the brave but battered 1980 British and Irish Lions Tour to South Africa, with political comment.

John's journalist ability to write a chronological sequence of facts and make it interesting, coupled to his telling pen portraits of people and places, make his book as technically sound and compulsive reading for rugby fiends as its predecessor, which covered the 1977 Lions tour to New Zealand.

Amongst the current proliferation of books on rugby and rugby tours, punters in W. H. SMITH's will probably place "The British Lions 1980" as one of the front runners in the browser's stakes, the number of photographs should ensure that. However like record stores can be alienating for people over 30, racial comment can be potentially alienating to could be purchasers of books about Rugby. In a strictly rugby context the 'political' comment is, as probably appropriate to the diary of a top of the tree rugby tour, as Ayer's rock is to the Australian desert.

One gets the feeling that the "political chapters" are the tangible evidence of the author's personal concern in having been seen to go to S. Africa. Maybe he should, maybe he shouldn't, have gone to S. Africa, but certainly a valid point of view is that he needn't have burdened the Rugby world at large with his guilty conscience. Appropriate and well written as they are, they maybe belong somewhere else.

Unless of course that is, like me, your a wishy washy liberal and the rest of the book can be seen as a well written filler around another wishy washy liberal's experiences in and of S. Africa.

John is now a golf correspondent.

"ONE MAN'S JOY IS ANOTHER MAN'S SORROW"

A few words written for the 1980, London Rugby Festival Programme

Welcome to the gig, Eric.

You may just be wondering what Rugby Union and their fat club ties are doing at Wonderful Wembley.

Hallowed Home of the Hungry He-Men from Rochdale Hornets, highstepping horses and highly over priced but not over paid international Kevins.

Well, Keith, wonder no more.

Instead.

Thrill to the names from Yesterday's Papers.

Rediscover your capacity for love by supporting the Met Police.

Espouse righteous causes like Richmond, Rosslyn Park, Harlequins and cliche dialogue.

Liberate your Lungs to the Good News from Toulouse.

An Iron Ovaries forward, from Idaho, charges a No Balls at All lady from Pittsburgh? in a 7-a-side tournament at Cleveland.

'SUFFER LITTLE CHILDREN'

Leer along with fab Bob Geldorf and the boys from Blackrock College and then live life on the margin — blah, blah, blah. 1965.

See the cut price battle scenes between Wasps and Blackheath.

Ignore potentially greater thrills by visiting the Sandpan when Rovigo are playing.

Keep an eye out for the catchpenny appeal of weird Andy Irvine and the good guys from Heriots Former Pupils.

Console yourself with the Metropolitan/Celtic charm of the boys in green.

Hustle yourself into three cups of ridiculously expensive Wembley Tea.

Swoon to the Saracens who have promised to provide a completely non-rivetting lack lustre performance.

Draw to the xenophobic chauvanistic delights of London Scottish.

The whole deal is guaranteed to be just as exacting as spending the morning at Sainsburys.

So welcome to the big deal of 1972, Shirley, I know you'll just love it.

An article sent to David Hards of The Times, who asked me to write all I know about the future of the game and all that blah, using both sides of the paper etc. etc. Something resembling this article was published in Spring '84.

Well it's very flattering as a occasional member of the Rosslyn Park 2nd XV to be asked by The Times rugby correspondent to write down my views, as a player, about my concerns about the future of the game of Rugby Football Union. Well, my main short term concern about the future of the game is how I can get back into the first XV, if training is compulsory every Tuesday and Thursday evening and I can't make Tuesday night as I've got to look after mouse and fruit popper, so Elisabeth can go to her aerobics class down the local church hall. Jane Fonda has a lot to answer for.

Also it doesn't follow because light years ago, one was lucky enough to play at a certain level one can now contribute or have any inside track on how the game should or could be organised in the 1990's. Cos one thing is certain that for the vast majority of rugby players, the collective huffing and puffing of the Rugby Football Union (R.F.U.), the International Board (I.B.), commercial interests, and even self opinionated ego trippers like me is going to have little material impact on their fun and enjoyment on a Saturday afternoon, which will depend solely on whether they still get a buzz out of the game.

The Future. The R.F.U. defender of a Victorian Sporting anachronism although recognising that they now control a potential multi-million pound revenue earning spectacle in the form of the National Team seem unwilling to me to promote it to its full potential for the benefit of the game, players, spectators and commercial interests. In 1984, International Rugby like all high revenue spectacles such as Wimbledon, International Cricket, the World Darts competition, a Duran – Duran concert have to varying degrees, everything to do with entertainment, talent, technical expertise, winning, politics and money, and little to do with sport. Sport is what you find in B String Club Athletics and sea fishing off Workington Pier on a Tuesday afternoon in January. All this is, in a way, a sadness for rugby since it implies a change in the status quo. However it's this change that the Rugby Football Union needs to adapt to. One of Rugby Football Unions problems once it eventually decides to adjust to underlying-changing circumstances is where to draw the line and more importantly why. At present by not yielding to the pressure of change, everyone knows exactly where they stand. By changing the structure the edifice crumbles, but so what, if where players and ex-players currently stand is becoming increasingly ludicrous. In my view there is absolutely no difference between my attitude towards the game, white knight for the moment and that of naughty boy Micky Burton. We both like rugby.

There is of course a cost involved in change. The cost would be a loss of something fairly intangible and its something to do with doing one's best, not being too concerned about numbers, enjoying oneself and making lifelong friends. Which is a heavy price but it's a certainty that it is less heavy than having the top end of the game hijacked by people whose sole interest is their immediate net profit.

A dog loves the man who feeds it. Players must be fed by the Union or through the Union so that the control, the rules and the structure is controlled by one respected powerful worldwide body, as has been the case to date.

Secondly, although the R.F.U. recognise and help to develop the game they seem unwilling to recognise that the game has also spread into areas where red never penetrated the globe. Hence the International Board offers only benign paternalism to the organisers and countries who play in the Hong Kong '7's and the comecon nations in Eastern Europe. When what these countries probably really want is the opportunity to play against and maybe beat the best in the world on a reasonably regular basis. No doubt they will keep a knocking for a while but if I was a Western Samoan or Russian administrator I'd get together with my local rugby playing chums and have a little competition of my own and yah boo sucks to the existing fuddy-duddy bodies in Britain and Ireland.

So what happens next in a changing world when South Africa is prepared to buy what it may not get for free, Australian Channel 9 needs more space filler between the ads, sports goods manufacturers need new personable clothes horses, cable stations and satellite T.V. will increasingly need product. In Maggie's brave new entrepreneurial world someone is going to put it together to the detriment of the control of the game unless the R.F.U. and I.B. don't get busy.

THE 1981 GRAND SLAM THINK TANK IN ACTION

SOME BARBARIANS IN HONG KONG

However, blinkered, tradition bound, it is sometimes suggested the R.F.U. maybe, they do genuinely care about the game. To use the old cliche their hearts are certainly in the right place. Having on a number of occasions met Bob Weighill, the secretary of the Rugby Football Union and through "Superstars" various sporting entrepreneurs I know who I'd like to be running and organising and controlling the game — no-one does it fairer than Big Bob.

However, the existing international bodies must take up not what they, I imagine, currently perceive as the threat, but the tremendous opportunities offered by commerce who are only looking for a good deal and also then give the game rather than ration it to the rest of the world. Because otherwise commerce and the world outside will take it away and the R.F.U.'s voice will be increasingly irrelevant to the development of the game. Which would be a shame.

So what could the R.F.U. do and suggest to the I.B. — well it could form a league system based on the major clubs, disband the current county structure, so that counties are fed by non major clubs and play against each other on a second tier level, form 4 major regional sides from the major clubs, change the 5 nations championship so that each 2nd year a world cup is staged on a geographically filtered basis and also allow players to cash in on their talents through their controlling bodies.

But hang on I hear fruit popper crying, maybe she's also concerned about the future of the game of rugby football or maybe it's something far more important like a wet nappy that needs changing.

Runners up
Plate losers
Quarter-finalists
Eliminated

Liverpool 1971
Ipswich 1972
Manchester 1972
Middlesex 1974

ART OF THE FLOWER OF ROSSLYN PARK c1975–82

NO MATTER HOW HARD THEY TRY YOU HAVE TO ADMIT THEY ARE AN UGLY LOT

CLUBS I'D LIKE TO BELONG TO

Croydon Orienteering Club

The Old Haileyburian Club

St. James's Gaslight Club

Royal Automobile Club

Stereoscoptic Society

British Legion

Winchcombe Women's Institute

Bovnik Whitney Appreciation Society

Pudding Club

2nd Para

Schedule D Case II

TITLES I'D LIKE TO BE GIVEN

Run of the Mill

Regular Jo

Man in the Street

Mr. Big

Top of the Tree

Lord Cobbold

Fife Fly Fishing Champion

Miss Nuneaton 1976

Eric

D.M. Forex Dealer

POSING 1975-85 SOMETIME MONEY LENDER

A PREMATURE OBIT. VOL 1.

Hong Kong Hilton Hotel, Saturday night 2nd April 1984, by now probably into morning. I realised, on my third vomit into the champagne bucket, I would start to look sad if I didn't go away.

Playing for the Public School Wanderers, well captaining actually, we'd done OK'ish, knocked out in the semi-finals by Fiji 12−4. Followed by a very good impression of group harmony of "The Wanderer" at the evening gig. Public School Wanderers was a bit of a misnomer really, 4 of us from comprehensives and Dave Pick fresh out of Cardiff Central: the Welsh James Dean of the 1980's.

Anyway there I was 36, with a busted knee. There are certain moments when you get a glimpse, this probably wasn't one of them, but this had to be the final fling, the end of the road, the closing of a chapter, etc, etc. No more invites to play somewhere exotic at someone else's expense. Perhaps the odd invite for a charity game at Esher or struggling to make Rosslyn Park 3rd XV.

I'd had a good run, first call from Mickey Steele-Bodger 1971 Grange Road, against Cambridge, last call Hong-Kong 1984 and lots of places in between.

Ten years older than David Johnstone, the next oldest player. I should be with Billy Beaumont leading a tour party, he seemed to be enjoying himself.

Lurched over the dance floor towards the green neon exit, Roger, whatever he's called, the Australian captain had bitten me on the bridge of my nose and blood was dripping down my shirt. I filled up an ash tray waiting for the lift, with vomit not blood. Found room 668. Put a wet flannel over my nose. Hit the dry heaves in the lavatory.

I know I'd do some athletics over the summer and some work on my knee. No-one was going to deny me more good times like this. Bob Hiller please keep playing you are my northern star.

SOME MORE BARBARIANS MASQUERADING AS PUBLIC SCHOOL
WANDERERS WHOEVER THEY ARE

A PREMATURE OBIT VOL. 2. AFGHANISTAN MAKES SENSE

Since I left the circus and became an older man,
Somewhere between leaving now and taking up my pension
plan,
I'll crouch on committees in my old club jacket,
Perhaps go into the Bank each day and maybe earn a packet.
'Cos when you're an ageing footballer you should take up
more sedentary sports
The truth is though, I look rather silly now, in my brand new
Addidas shorts.
Perhaps I'll trade in my boots and try some after luncheon
dozing,
And hang around Wimbledon golf club and do some middle
aged posing,
Oh life will have its compensations, of that you can have no
fear,
'Cos its better to be 36 in England that 18 in Eritrea.

MY STORY (IT'S FAB)

Getcha hankies out kids.

This is the sad one.

A tale of deprivation and hardship in the aspiring lower middle classes and a young boy from a split home and a large family desperately vertically integrating upwards through society.

A rugby ball firmly under one arm.

You're gonna love it.

It's a winner.

Numero Uno.

Enid Archer, eat your heart out.

Once upon a time a long long time ago in December 1947, in darkest Liverpool in the depths of the coldest winter since the BBC Meteorological Office first started keeping records, a small cry was heard.

It was me.

I was born the youngest of five (2 boys, 3 girls).

The 1947 Education Act.

Marshall Aid.

The welfare programmes of the post World War Two Bevan government.

Bretton Woods

And Uncle Mac

Were big contributors to giving the world the economic, social and political freedom of the 1960's.

My mum,

Jessie, is now 76,

and is and has always been fab.

In the days when I suppose if you want to qualify for the title of being a nice person (which I desperately aspire to) then you've got to love your Mum.

Well I do.

My Dad

He's 83 and at 83 everyone deserves a mention.

Born in 1901.

In the trenches at the end of World War One, so he says. An engineer in the merchant navy.

Married in 1937.

Joined up in 1939.

Every two years on leave

Which is why there is two years between each brother and sister.

Mum and Dad too independent to live together and the cold congealed egg yolk on his tie.

They separated.

Me now, aged 7.

The family moved to Bristol.

Mick (16) left school (Quarry Bank — his claim to fame) and got a job as a trainee clerk in the Accident Department of New Scotland Yard

Which is why he always said he'd never ride a motor-bike.

He lived in a hostel, where he learnt to play cards.

It's a tear jerker.

Back in Bristol my Mum and her sister whose husband had recently died bought a house in Westbury Park with their father.

Grandad,

Who had fought in the Boer War and was very very old and wise.

My Mum was a primary school teacher.

I didn't see my father again until I was 13.

When my eldest sister, Jacky, was about to marry Frank who is Ghanaian,

He came home with the memorable words. "I didn't fight through two World Wars to have my daughter marry some black bastard", and a gun.

He fired a shot into the carpet.

If you don't believe me you can ask my sister Eileen.

Then he left.

Actually,

My Dad has mellowed a lot since.

He's now the scourge of the meals on wheels ladies in Gloucestershire.

Periodically little kids come and ring his doorbell
And he comes out and growls at them.

He phones me every Sunday and is full of cliched but, nevertheless, good advice

Like — enjoy yourself 'cos you're a long time dead.

Frank's still alive too.

Mum provided a background of love and of caring for each other and hopefully other people.

My childhood was O.K.

And so's my family.

Bully for me.

My Comprehensives

1953 – 55	Springwood Infant School	–	Liverpool
1956 – 59	Westbury Park Junior School	–	Bristol
1959 – 66	Greenway Comprehensive School	–	Bristol

I can't remember anything about Springwood Infants School apart from nature walks and kicking a tennis ball in the school yard.

Westbury Park Junior School was wonderful although I didn't adjust too well to the move and they did sums in a different way. I was in the middle of the A Forms and played football for the school team.

1959 was the year Bristol really threw money at comprehensive education. It was the year I took my 11+, I wanted to go to one of the smart grammar schools, with my brother and sisters (apart from Lois that is, who had failed her 11+, elitist education is great, provided you're in the elite) but I was sent to Greenway Comprehensive School for Boys, Southmead. I cried my little heart out.

Southmead is a modern industrial estate, an 8 or 8a bus ride away from the more genteel bedsits of Redland.

Where we lived we were the first grammar stream to go into what was an already established secondary modern school.

That's were I first learnt about labels — if you caught a bus to school you were a snob and it was open season on snobs. So 7th September 1959 about 30 of us turned up with new satchels, caps, ties, blazers and polished shoes, like lambs to the slaughter. Little did we know that school uniform was not new satchels, caps, ties, blazers and polished shoes.

Well you learnt pretty quickly about the herding instinct and not to wear your cap in public and if anyone in Redland asked you where you went to school, an indistinct mumble or a straightforward lie came in pretty handy.

The aim of comprehensive education was to develop the talents of each pupil whatever the level of physical, intellectual, artistic or practical ability and the comprehensive school was to provide the framework for doing that. Now I'm sure that's the objective of any educationalist. However, the difference with comprehensive education was that the door was ostensibly open to everyone. Also the appropriate level of education could vary over time rather than deciding at one chronological point in time at say 11+ and a dividing into sheep and goats for ever. Tough on the chimeras.

The idea has got to be acceptable and in 1959, local councils had the money to, in part, overcome the obvious problems. The teaching staff were enthusiastic, reasonably well paid (I think) and motivated. We had new equipment, new laboratories, metal and wood working rooms and a cinder running track.

After the second year we were taken out of our little clique of grammar stream boys and put in house tutorial groups of varying ages and abilities. Teaching groups were still based on academic performance. I don't know whether it worked. I left in 1966. By 1970 the wind of economic change was beginning to be felt.

I'm sure they didn't offer a course in Economics "A" level for 2 people after 1970. Cutbacks must have had their influence on teacher morale and there had always been an underlying current of violence which if it wasn't harnessed could only result in mindless aggravation.

Not that it's a measure of anything but eight of us got University Places in 1966, I don't know whether anyone else ever did. Greenway Comprehensive School closed down on 20th July 1984.

Amongst lots of other things I played rugby a couple of times in my last year at school.

A cautionary tale on the buying of second hand cars

June 1966 "A" levels out of the way. I'd been growing my hair over my collar like everyone else for the last couple of years. I'd had a morning paper round since I'd been 14 and what with bits and pieces had bought myself a BSA Bantam 125 and later had a single pot BSA 500cc (given to me by the metalwork master). Which was strange as I really wanted a Lambretta Ld 150 and a Green Fur Lined Parka, a pair of desert boots, well faded levis, a checked button down shirt and to walk up and down St Ives beach listening to the Top 20 on the light programme on Sunday afternoon. Anyway this was not to be because when I passed my driving test, I bought a 1934 Hillman for £30. This gave me great face driving to school (collecting petrol money) and going to the White Hart Pub on a Saturday night prior to gate crashing parties in Stoke Bishop where the conversation revolved around who was upstairs with whom. Anyway this relic wasn't up to a canoeing trip to N. Cornwall and it died on the A38, although it had been to Llandovery for a trip down the River Teifi and Towey. Anthea Stait said I looked like Paul Jones. I looked in the mirror a lot. But then again I hadn't heard Ray Davies's words of wisdom about looking more like we are if we didn't use the mirror so often. That summer I decided to work and buy a proper car. Jobs were easy to get. I got a job working at Hosegoods Silo, Avonmouth, sweeping up the dust in the warehouse, created by the conveyer belts taking the grain from the ship to the silo and then from the silo to the road shute.

Clock in at eight, work till five or maybe six, if you could get the overtime, usually working Saturdays and Sundays if you were lucky and a ship wanted to turn around quickly. I even worked August bank holiday − double pay and a day in lieu. I worked throughout that lovely Small Faces and Who summer from the middle of June to the end of September 1966.

I was really mean. I used to spend hours working out that if I bought a Mars Bar it was equivalent to about 7 minutes of my life that wasn't a good deal so I didn't buy it or anything, but it gave me something to think about, while I was sweeping up.

By the end of September 1966 I had saved, misered more like, about £450 which was then the cost of a new mini-van or a one year old Triumph Spitfire. Did I buy a new mini-van? No I bought a 2½ litre, fastback, tinted windows 140mph, with a wood and aluminium trimmed steering wheel with twin Weber carburettors 1956 Lancia Aureilia GT. It looked fantasic. I don't know much about cars. It was a heap. You've got to judge a man by the size of his carburettors.

I drove it to the University of East Anglia, first year residences at Horsham Saint Faith, it died. Jack the Burke. At the end of the first term only having first and fourth gear I drove it back to Bristol and sold it for £80. I've never had any interest in flashy cars since September 1966.

1966–1969

Made it. Got to University just like my elder brother. I doubt whether I would today. However, in the 60's someone had had the idea of increasing the number of University places to cope with the post World War Two population bulge. Thank you whoever that was. So they built at different speeds half a dozen new Universities on a loose course assessment and American campus basis.

Now I'd like to say that 18–21 in anyone's life must be a golden time but that isn't the case. Aged 18, male in 1914 in any W. European country must have been miserable, aged 18 living in Coventry, can't get a job, no hope, must be pretty mediocre.

However, to be young, at the University of East Anglia 1966–69 during that period of social change, was to be at the centre of the universe. A stage to play a role, relative financial independence, friends if you wanted them (I did, I did), something to do once in a while to give you a reason for being there. It was too good to be true. Of course it wasn't truth or reality it was terrific fun and self delusion based on the government and taxpayers' generosity, music and a forever rainbow future with Vietnam as a convenient backdrop. But if that was self delusion give me more. My friends then are my friends now, although I never see them.

POP. Out of the education machine in July 1969. 21 years old and my character and attitudes were formed. Milky White wishy washy liberal, self effacing, keen to appreciate the other man's point of view.

I've only made a couple of consequential (to me) journeys which I paid for myself and I have recounted one in detail, it's now prehistoric, but I remember it all.

The U.S.A. Summer 1968

During the year 1968, I was the University of East Anglia's Rag Chairman, not something you'd really want to shout from the roof tops. It was ultimately, I suppose, a cock up and didn't raise that much money. In my defence it was the first year it had been tried. We combined with the local art college and teachers training college and put on lots of do's during a week of the summer term — to name drop but a few — Ravi Shankar, the Dubliner's, Ten Years After, The Marmalade, Dave, Dee, Dozy etc. The big deal was an open air rock concert on the outskirts of Norwich. You remember open air rock concerts. Well, what they didn't have at Woodstock on the big day was torrential rain. I can distinctly remember getting back from this minor fiasco and hearing the flowerpot men singing on Radio Caroline, "Lets Go to San Francisco" so I thought that's got to be better than drowning in Norfolk. I was a prat.

Here I am aged 22, with a smashing left knee, no long scar under my left eye and only one broken finger, and all my own teeth

Although the government of the day had undertaken major health, education and road building programmes, they were out to lunch on the jolly old Balance of Payments on Current Account. As a consequence of which tourists could only take £50 on holiday.

So there I was 1968 sitting on a B.U.N.A.C. charter aircraft. £50 in my pocket en route for New York. The summer migrations of the great unwashed, thousands of us did it — anyway this is my story John.

The plane depressurised somewhere over Greenland, if you don't believe me ask Wendy Taylor she was sitting next to me. I suppose it's many people's nightmare to be on a plane that's dropping out of the sky, its certainly one of mine, other nightmares usually are about the dark and being in murky waters. Anyway the plane levelled out at a few thousand feet, much to everyone's relief, especially mine and Wendy Taylor's. She was 19, at Hull University and going to work in a paint factory in Long Island where she had relatives. We swopped addresses, a habit I am trying to break.

B.U.N.A.C. gave you one free night at the Sheraton Hotel, 5th Avenue (No less) however, by shifting rooms you could spin it out a bit longer. £50 is what your average New York window cleaner used to earn in a bad few days.

I got a bus out of New York and stood by the side of the road on Interstate Highway 78. I'm given to understand that in the U.S.A. nowadays only muggers and gays hitch and they only get picked up by muggers and gays and this leads to abused dead bodies and the police don't like cleaning up the mess so they've made hitching illegal. In 1968 I know hitching was illegal in Washington State because a policeman put me on a bus and I think it was illegal in Colorado. However, in '68 I got lifts from Mute Mexicans, Old Ladies, Weirdos, Students, Married Couples, Gays, etc, etc and not necessarily in that order.

Anyway there I was getting small short rides from nice people along the highway when a big black car stopped and I got a ride from 3 1968 American freaks who had dropped out of the University of Chicago and like me and the rest of the world were heading for California. They let me ride with them if I paid a quarter of the petrol it was a good business arrangement, they drove in turn non stop, after a day and a half we were in Amarillo Texas on Highway 66 (very Rolling Stones). I got out, not because I was running out of money or because I was concerned their car was like a travelling drug shop (they intended selling tabs of acid, to get by and they had enough for the whole of Los Angeles), but because I'd seen nothing of America.

I suppose I ought to mention something about drugs. Legalistics aside, in the 60's/70's, drugs were taken to expand the vision and other such crap. In the 1980's drugs are taken to block things out, neither is worth messing your body up for.

If you have a drug problem and you can't afford to feed it then you have a real problem. The Exiled Iranians have a lot to answer for. School kids on drugs or sniffing are a tragedy and the really sad thing is they can't see it.

Anyway where was I. Oh Yes Amarillo. The only time I caught a Greyhound it was late and I went to Denver, where a U.E.A. American exchange student Jim Brandt lived.

I stayed for a week, we had a great time he was at summer school in Boulder in the foothills of the Rockies. Although all I can really remember is hearing a version of "Young Girl" by Gary Puckett and the Union Gap on a car radio that had a month or so earlier been a hit for "the Precious Few" in the UK.

Through the classified ads of the Denver Post I got myself a job washing up in a Dude Ranch in Evergreen Colorado. It was in a beautiful setting. The guests after coffee, grits and pancakes would ride the trails periodically being met by a ranch pick up truck that would give them more coffee, grits and pancakes, then they'd come back to the ranch and have breakfast. This generated lots of washing up. In fact I wasn't washer up I was assistant to the washer up. Who was about 30 and very macho and didn't like me around as it queered his pitch with the other two assistant but female kitchen helps.

At the end of a long week of having the cleanest hands in the world, we assistants went to a concert at Red Rocks, which was miles away. In Colorado if you're under 21 you can/could only drink, what is called 3.2 beer, which I think refers to the alcoholic content, it is sold in pitchers and tastes like lemonade. I drank lots. It's 5000 feet up. Surfacing very late the following morning I got G.B.H. of the ear from Macho and there I was walking down the road back to Denver and Jim Brandt but now at least with a few dollars.

I then got a job as a rodeo guard, so I bid my farewells and headed to downtown Denver. They didn't have my size rodeo guard's outfit. So I caught a bus and hitched to Laramie, then Salt Lake City and down through to Nevada. I don't remember much apart from people being very friendly which is surprising as I was sleeping by the side of the road. However, it was warm and the cowboys slept out.

I arrived in Las Vegas about midnight and had this idea of trying to get a ride so I wouldn't frizzle in the desert — I was so dumb.

Now if you've ever hitched to avoid the tedium you'll know how you invent games like; I'll wait for ten cars; or; until a quarter past and if I haven't got a lift then I'll walk to another place or I'll put on a clean shirt, or whatever. Anyway there I was about one in the morning hitching, counting the infrequent cars, when one of them stopped.

I got in, we traded information, he's 27, Argentinian works in a casino, I'm me etc, after about 5 minutes he says he's not going far but if I'd like to I can come back with him and clean up. Now maybe I'm totally stupid but anything (well almost) is better than a Nevadan ditch and I do smell and maybe the poodle should have warned me. So I lock the door have a shower and then for the first time think. Now what is to stop him from saying I'd broken into his house and then shooting me. Or less dramatically maybe he'll burst in on me and News-of-the-World-about-page-six-me. I open the door and he's standing there in his jeans and he says "Can you take Photographs?" I am at this stage petrified. He notices this and tells me not to worry I can stay the night and no strings or he'll take me back to where he picked me up. I asked him to take me back.

Once out of the house and in relatively common ground in his car I realise I'm about a foot taller and 80lbs heavier. I'm now relieved and he's very kind. He tells me (1968 remember) that the problem of being gay is the social alienation associated with it and as I was hitching he assumed I was familiar with gays as hitch hikers were his usual source of casual partners and if I'd never tried it why not try it now. I think I said something which probably sounded like my acceptance of consenting adults behind closed doors etc, etc, but the thought of me being one of those adults didn't have any appeal. As I got out of his car he said "Take it easy Andrew not everyone's as nice as I am".

Two o'clock and I gratefully keeled over into the ditch. Sunrise and a very wrinkled old lady in an enormous car drove me all the way to Orange County.

Los Angeles, well California was full of illusion chasers like me. I went through Los Angeles quickly in 1968. I was there in '73 with the England Rugby Team and then in '78 with Paris University Rugby Club. It's nice.

I remember well the beach at Ventura, in the evening with my head on my bag and my jacket done up watching the sun dropping down below the sea. Getting a ride was difficult as there were so many of us I even took to putting a Union Jack on the side of my bag. Up Highway 101, I spent a night in an army barracks at a language tuition centre in Monterey and had breakfast courtesy of the U.S. armed forces.

Then I got a ride from some guy to San Jose. He was very kind. He'd been in Europe the year before and it was my good fortune to be the recipient of his goodwill. He got me a job for two weeks painting a roundabout in a kiddies playpark that was attached to a local supermarket. A couple of years ago I worked for Stanford Research Institute in Menlo Park just north of San Jose, I hired a car to go and see him, but he was long gone.

"Let's go to San Francisco" might have been the spark but what a let down. I thought Haight-Ashby was riddled with aggravation. Love and Peace, I didn't see much evidence, besides which I now had a few dollars. Having a few quid in your pocket gives you a different perspective than being totally broke.

I spent a couple of days drifting up through N. California, Oregon and Washington State and on in to Vancouver. Where I met two girls hitching in the main street, they asked me back to where they were staying. It was a nice place, varnished wooden floors, no furniture and about 12 other assorted vagrants, probably most of them, like me, are now Chartered Accountants. Getting the rent together was the big deal, some people sold the Georgia Straight 7½ cents wholesale 15 cents retail (Last year I spoke at the Vancouver Rowing Club 75th anniversary, I learnt the Georgia Straight is now anything but) some went begging, I couldn't do that, too proud. Although give me some real poverty instead of playing at it and I reckon I could. I think someone's parents sent a cheque. It was late July.

I got a lift on to the Trans-Canadian highway but I obviously didn't get that far as I landed up that evening at a U.S./Canadian crossing point just east of the Cascade Mountains, I curled up on a plank under the one street light something was howling and there were enormous flying bugs that kept crashing into the stanchion holding up the light. I then drifted down through Idaho, Montana and Wyoming and finished up spending a few days in Yellowstone. The states are beautiful but especially Wyoming and Colorado as the Rockies drop into the plains.

I then got another job for 3 weeks, painting up condominiums in Breconridge, getting them ready for the Colorado Winter Ski Season. It was a good job and suddenly I was rich I got a bus through Colorado Springs, Kit Carson Park and to Los Alamos (atomic city), New Mexico. Where I stayed with a guy who had been a U.K./U.S. exchange student. I stayed a week and it was the time of the Sante Fe festival, which brings together the Mexican, Spanish, Indian and American cultures. Then back to hitching through New Mexico to El Paso. It cost a penny to cross the Rio Grande, I thought I might head to Chihuahua but Mexico is poor, you don't get rides and I was carrying a couple of hundred dollars, I got a bus back to El Paso.

I then got one ride right across Texas, with a guy who was about to go to Vietnam, to Fort Worth. Then I got picked up by a bloke who had California plates who felt he was risking life and limb driving through the Northern tip of the Southern States, Lousianna, Mississippi, Alabama to Georgia. I got out at Augusta. My elder brother Mick, after going back to school had got a doctorate in Geology and had spent sometime looking for kaolin in Georgia. I didn't find any and I didn't find him.

Anyway this is now sounding like a travelogue to wrap it up, I spent a week sunbathing on Virginia Beach, headed up through the Eastern States, bought a hi-fi in 42nd Street and 20 or so records, spent a celibate week on Long Island with Wendy Taylor and her relatives and flew home thinking I had my finger on the pulse. Which of course I did.

Summer 1969 Afghanistan but not India

Out of University (before a job) I hitched to Greece and then caught buses across long tracks of land. Life was cheap. Getting there and back was just a matter of survival. I don't remember it as being much fun.

PELL MELL

Andy Ripley, the former England and British Lions rugby player, competed in this year's Superstars competition in the U.S. and did much of this training at the Pall Mall clubhouse. Here he recounts what happened to him after he had finished third in the final.

Was it McLuhan in the good old 1960's who pointed out that if it's on TV then it's important. Presumably it also follows if it's not on TV it's not important. Anyway, it was interesting that suddenly after the transmission, I achieved some sort of notoriety. It was marvellous. There I was, Mr. No-one from Nowhere, well actually Andrew Ripley from Liverpool, but for about two weeks I momentarily had an inkling what it would be like to be Reggie or Kevin. However, like my ten-month-old son's attention which can last only for about 20 seconds on any one person or thing, after all too short a time I noticed that no longer was I recognised in the menswear counter of Marks and Sparks in Nuneaton. A tragedy.

MUGSHOT OF A SUPERSTAR (ED-NOTE OH YEH?)

SUPERTEAM

SUPERSTAR

SUPERMAN

Although between you and me, if you have an option on being the window on which the sun glints for a moment then two weeks of notoriety is just about the optimum period. The world, in the shape of various journalists, comes to your door and you can hold forth on matters which five minutes ago you probably had no opinion whatsoever and they get it all down and pay for lunch. Publishers ask if you can write a book and you even get considered for appearing on Punchlines with Lennie Bennett. Terrific. Well actually it was. My mum is now being considered as a possible contender for the Presidency of Winchcombe's Women's Institute. She is over the moon.

My approach to the competition was fairly similar to the way I prepared for school examinations. I tried to delude whoever I was trying to delude that I could do well in spite of the fact that I was extremely lazy. The reality being to study/run my little socks off whenever I thought the deludees weren't watching. In other words, for God's sake succeed, but don't be seen to be trying.

Contestants are barred from competing in their speciality event. This usually works to the particular disadvantage of track athletes. It also means that the actual level of attainment is usually less than world shattering. The programme doesn't have much to contribute to sporting excellence but it does give an insight into known sports figures' personalities in competitive situations. Neither is it just a case of, see-the-hero-fall-on-the-banana-skin. Or is it?

I found particularly interesting the finished product and the events. The events have a sort of school sports day feel about them. However, if you put them into a framework of a professional BBC film crew, credible presenters and a skilled cutting/editing team, then the end-product tends to lose its amateur, on the spot, feel and to look like what it is, a well presented polished hour of sports related entertainment.

The best aspect as a competitor was not the competition (although that was always 100%) but meeting the other competitors and getting a feel, although probably a totally distorted one, for other sports. Cliché that it sounds, it didn't matter (for that moment anyway) that on one side was a millionaire ex-racing driver from Monte Carlo playing against an Irish canoeist, who well knows his way around UB40. What was important was who was best at jumping over an obstacle course.

For me Superstars was a nice little window on a different world and added a certain passing sparkle.

Hi, Jacques – how's your political future these days?
AGR receives the Freedom of Paris from the Mayor M. Chirac

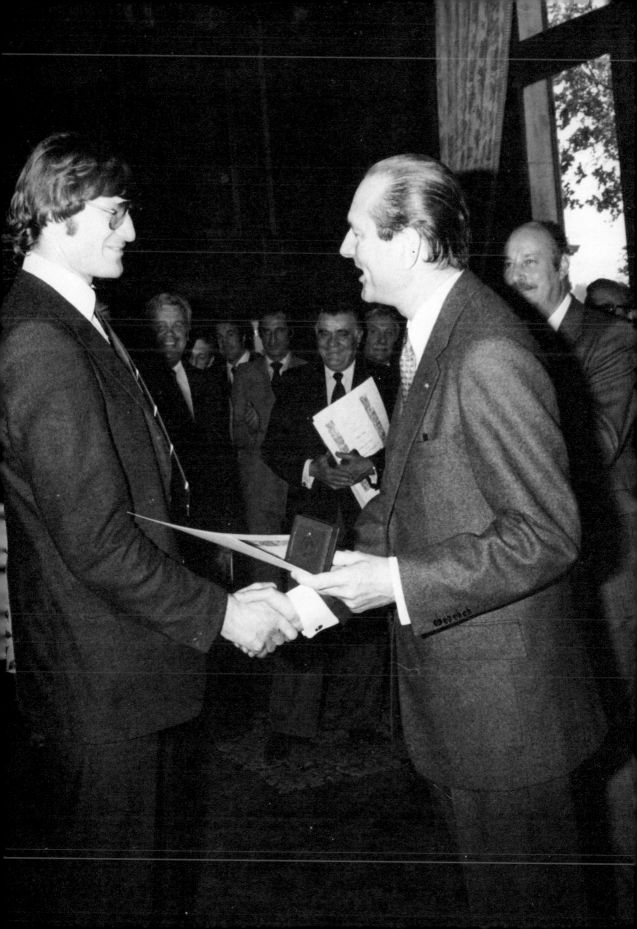

THOMAS HARDLY ORIGINAL

The Rugby Football Union is now defunct.
There was a time when we could talk relevancies and agree,
in five minutes
one
two
three
four
five
Jesus that was a beautiful time.
and now Doctor Death what do you think of your beautiful game?

Stolen from E.J. Thribb who stole it from a famous person.

the subtle footwork of Richard Moriarty

Money

Money is what we need because:

Life is miserable if you haven't got any.

Life can also be miserable if you've got too much and live in Italy and have kidnappable kith and kin. However, as most of us aren't Italian, too much money isn't too big a problem.

How much do you need?:

Enough to get by. This is, however, a problem since getting by means different things to different people.

Money & Delusion:

Once I have £X (dollars/yen/etc) saved I can pay off the HP on the motor-bike, mortgage on the house, retire, go back-packing in Western Samoa, blah, blah, blah. Until that time, I will carry on with my humble existence, but when I've got £X I can really live rainbows, sunshine and daisies.

If you get £X, you'll need £X + 1.

Why do you need money?:

1. To live.

2. To show off.

P.S. Our society is based on money. If you've got it then you'll be O.K.

There's a problem with the measurement of U.S. dollars these days

There's an industry, or two or four or eight,
of academic economists, growing at an exponential rate.
Desperately discussing the changing value of money over time.
Trying to evaluate what is their's or your's or mine.

Discussing the velocity with which dollar notes change hands.
Refining the changing definitions of various monetary bands,
Accommodating to varying degrees different inflation rates,
Allowing for the changing value of currencies in different national
states.

Oh it's a dynamic melee of stochastic variables,
all making the accounting equations even more unbearable
But really it's pretty straightforward and could even be called plain
But unfortunately no-one's got a ruler in this high stakes financial
game.

Because even though everyone in the whole world seems to be skint,
There's a few things they don't want, like for example, the good old
Hungarian Forint.

However,
If I'm a Russian hooker at an FX Intourist hotel, what do I want?
U.S. Dollars
If I'm selling an Argentinian hacienda, what do I want?
U.S. Dollars.
If I'm a Columbian Cocaine dealer, what do I want?
U.S. Dollars
If I'm an Abu Dhabi Oil Co-operative Council Member, what do I want?
U.S. Dollars.
If I'm a Nigerian customs official, what do I want?
U.S. Dollars.
If I'm an Israeli orange salesman, what do I want?
U.S. Dollars.

And so this growth of the U.S. fiduciary issue has continued to spread,
Accurately counted by no-one, not even the good old Fed.
So the Fed put up dollar interest rates to suck it all back home,
Desperate to cool inflation as the U.S. economy starts to groan.

Now real growth plus interest rates equals the allowed growth in
money supply
While U.S. Government expenditure, less tax, keeps the deficit at an all
time high
But the Fed, who may not be able to quantify, are also not corruptible
Aren't too concerned with U.S. interest rates, 'cos for U.S. citizens
they're tax deductible.

If the U.S. Government just prints the notes, to fund the deficit, so the
story goes,
Inflation will become rampant and supply side economists will die and
decompose.
But who's measuring the dollars that slipped out the back door
and are daily used in external U.S. transactions from here to Singapore.

So go on Ron, help Mexico, Brazil, Yugoslavia, the Deutsch Mark, Yen
and Sterling,
You can do your bit for us all by just setting those printing presses
whirling.

As a side hopeful:

*You can see the stars line up at the back door for their dose
of brown envelopes and humiliation. Just like the dockers used
to do at the Royal Docks. You can choose which one works and which
one doesn't. Power and Money, it's gotta be fun, fun, fun.*

don't delay, call today.

PRO SPORTS INTERNATIONAL LTD

TEMPUS FUGIT KIDDO

It's a drip, drip, drip
It's a chip, chip, chip
When I race in the 400 metres hurdles next Saturday it will
be Southern League, division 4 match at Chiswick Cinder Track
Never so grand again, as at my peak of athletic achievement.
When I failed to qualify for the AAA final in 1978.
Oh golden days when I was ranked 35th in the country.
35th in the whole of the U.K.
You can touch me if you want.
Join the queue.
On Saturday at Chiswick I race against my ghosts.

1972 –	54.9
1973 –	55.2
1974 –	54.5
1975 –	55.7
1976 –	55.1
1977 –	54.6
1978 –	53.7
1979 –	54.3
1980 –	55.2
1981 –	54.9
1982 –	55.6
1983 –	56.2
1984 –	57.2

It's a drip, drip, drip
It's a chip, chip, chip

My first
and only marathon
3 hrs 52 mins

UNFUNNY T-SHIRT SLOGANS

DUVETS ALTERED

PICK RASPBERRIES
IN SYRIA

MY DAD IS GAY

MARRIAGE GUIDANCE
COUNSELLOR

CRISIS. WHAT CRISIS?

I AM NOT A FISH

I AM NOT
ROBIN LEIGH-PEMBERTON

Can Rock Stars still act
like adolescents when they are
suffering from mid life crises?

People will believe
you are what you appear
to be

Hello I'm just a
red headed, Irish, wine loving,
tennis playing, garlic eating
wind surfing actor/
writer called Mohammed

I hate Graffiti,
in fact I can't stand any
Italian food

MY MUM

My Mum is 76.

My Mum.

She has 5 children, fourteen grandchildren and a bad left shoulder,

My Mum.

Last year she went down the Nile with her friend, Aggie and didn't get diarrhea.

She's smart, my Mum

She was a primary school teacher and brought five of us up on her own.

My Mum.

She gave birth to Jacky during an air raid in Liverpool in 1941,

My Mum.

As kids **My Mum** loved us all equally,

My Mum.

My Mum plays tennis, bowls and likes going for long walks.
   When Eileen was into puberty, my Mum was involved in the menopause,

   There was friction.

   They're as close as mother and daughter could ever be now.

   When my Mum was 68, she lived in Australia for 3 months with my brother.

   When my Mum was 70, she lived in Hong Kong for 3 months with my sister.

   When my Mum was 71, she went to California for 3 months with Mrs. Davies.

   My Mum is amazing, she lives on a state pension (separated women) and a half teachers' pension (didn't teach during her 30's as she was always having babies) and yet she's always catching aeroplanes.

My Dad has given her £50 a month since the time when £50 was £50.

After 18 years of separation in 1970 when the fledglings had flown the Bristolian nest and my Dad had blown up the S.S. Castledore in Madras, Mum and Dad tried to live together.

To grow old and grow roses.

After eighteen months, one night in November, my Mum decided enough was enough. Aged 66 got into her clapped out Austin 1100 and left.

My Mum.

The car broke down just after midnight on the M4.

My Mum can do anything My Mum can.

My Mum could win an Olympic medal in the 100 metres men's freestyle in Seoul and she doesn't even like swimming.

My Mum.

When I or my brother or sisters fall, she's always there to pick us up, like she always has done.

My Mum.

I never tell her I love her because, well,

She's My Mum.

My Niece

Yesterday I saw my niece
in a theatre production at the Oval Arts Centre.
It was not a play. Neither was it Iolanthe.
She's a beneficiary of a GLC grant for a black woman's theatre group.
With an uncle's eye, I was proud.
She's 21 and she can stand up and say
I'm a woman
and I'm black.
Though there's nothing too remarkable about that.
It's obvious.
Really.
I think she thinks she's dangerous.
I wanted to be dangerous once.
On balance, I think I'd prefer to see her in Iolanthe.

When I'm running along the Embankment.
It surprised me when I read John Lennon voted Conservative.
I plod along and dream.
"All I am saying is give peace a chance".
I'm safe in me and the adrenalin is flowing.
Seems to be the anthem of the peace movement.
Two men don't get out of my way.
I now wonder about "God Save the Queen".
Don't they realize this is my pavement.
Was it written by a Marxist-Leninist?
I want to smash them.
Still who cares?
And I'm gone.
(The hand that turns this page will be a skeleton's hand one day. T. Hee)
I feel ridiculous — till the next time.

MY LITTLE KIDLETS

I'm 36 years and 52 days old next Wednesday

I owe £115,000

I have just under £10,000 in the Conventry Building Society

I have part of a converted house in Lingfield

I have part of a semi-detached house in Fulham, which no-one wants to buy

I've been married for 8 years

I begin to look my age

I have no secrets from the Inland Revenue.

I have two sunbeams that dance on my head at six in the morning.

I love them.

STAND UP AND FIGHT

I've always loved Boxers.
Sometimes it seems, the more vicious the game,
the gentler the man.
Perfect lumps of dancing meat surrounded by creeps on a percentage.
Mohammed Ali seems to be all the evidence
that the British Medical Association needs to present its case.
He wouldn't have had it any other way.
He's lucky.
He got rich n' famous.

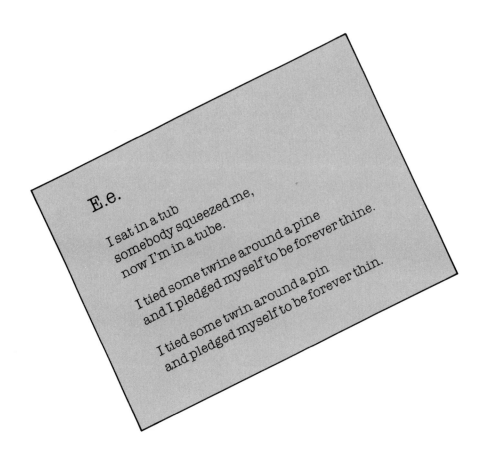

E.e.

I sat in a tub
somebody squeezed me,
now I'm in a tube.

I tied some twine around a pine
and I pledged myself to be forever thine.

I tied some twin around a pin
and pledged myself to be forever thin.

WHO ARE THESE PEOPLE?

Gervieve Jumblatt

Lee Bum Souk

Cannan Banana

George Ripley

PILLOW TALK

Said Estrogen to Testerone

'I must go down the disco'

Said Testerone to Estrogen

'Is that in Southampton or San Francisco?'

Said Estrogen to Testerone

'Don't be so silly, you know it's in Crawley, you big dope!'.

William Webb Ellis
with a fine
disregard for the
rules of football...
...first took the
ball in his arms
and ran with it.

WHADYA MEAN PRETENTIOUS?

So it is with man; Helpless in his infancy.

Communicable and incorruptible,

Finding joy in seeing emphasised the second of five syllables.

Extravagantly wild in his youth.

Leading to an inevitable drift towards accenting the middle syllable generating only contradiction and consternation.

Superficial speculation, copulation and peer uniformity being the hallmarks of emphasising the middle syllable of five.

To the final state.

Where the accent is upon the third syllable from the end, and is full of miseries.

No communication, total dilapidation, occasional humiliation.

Friends betray him, wrongs oppress him

His time a span, himself a bubble, of just two syllables.

TONGUE OF THE MONTH

1.

2.

3.

4.

1   ROGER SHACKLETON

2   CHARLES RALSTON

3   FRED PERRY

4   GOOD EVANS

5.

6.

9.

7.

8.

5 MAURICE

6 FLASHER

7 FORMER SECOND ROW

8 MIKE GIBSON MARK 1 VERSION

9 HANDY

10 ME

11 MARCUS ROSE IN DRAG

11.

FINALIST

4.

3.

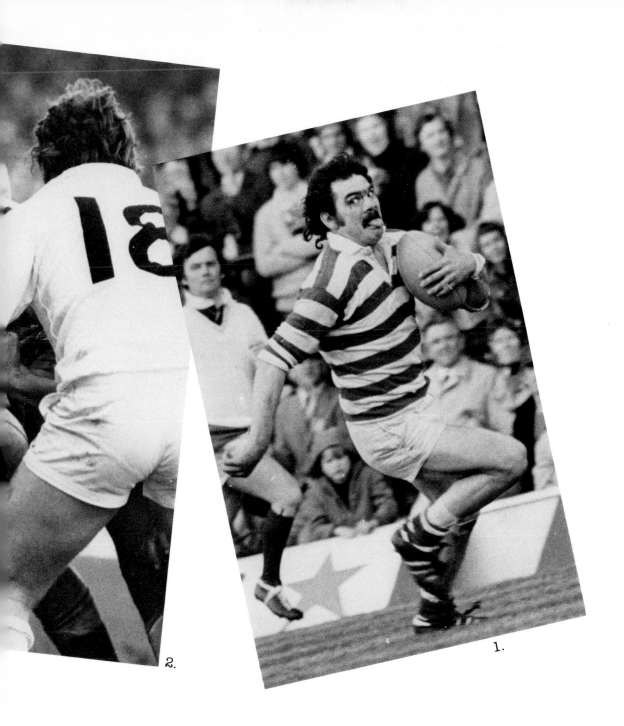

2.   1.

4   MARK 1 AGAIN

3   LE FLY HALF

2   BAMBER GASGOINE

AND
1   THE WINNER

18TH OCTOBER 1901 – 9TH DECEMBER 1984

When I put this, for want of a better word, book together in August 1984 it was only to be, what it appears to be, that is the result of two weeks of collecting bits and pieces of scribble together and thumbing through old photographs. It was pure self indulgence on my part and maybe as my excuse for doing it, it would make a few quid for the N.S.P.C.C. I also included a few words on my family, 'cos they're interesting and we love each other.

Almost at the last stages of production, my Dad died. Out of respect I felt I ought to change a few references I had made about him.

Death makes everyone a hero.

But, I didn't.

"But Dad you were a difficult man. I'd only met you in my 20's and early 30's and by then you were in your 70's and 80's. They said you had a temper and were selfish, maybe you were; and I've no doubt that you're now knocking seven bells out of the grim reaper.

But Dad you were always smart. Leaving your money equally to your 14 grandchildren now aged between one and twenty-one was a good idea. Because for the next 20 years there are going to be 14 sets of questions. Who was he? What did he do? Well I'll tell them, Dad. You were born at the turn of the century in Nun Muncton in Yorkshire and your farming family fell on hard times. So when you were small your father pulled a hand cart with you and your three sisters to Lincolnshire where he worked until he died as an itinerant farm labourer. You were your mother's darling − they said she spoilt you. You went to sea at 14 and for the next 53 years you sailed everywhere. There was no port that you hadn't seemed to have visited, no language you hadn't heard and no wisdom you hadn't acquired. You served in two wars as a merchant seaman and had two ships torpedoed from under you. You made it to be Chief Engineer on luxury passenger ships on the North Atlantic run. Then at 59, you were made redundant by Cunard. At 60 you were given another ticket for a further seven years as Chief of a tramp steamer which eventually blew up in Madras. Then, you came home. You and mum tried to live together again, but it didn't work and you became a character in the village. You 'phoned me every Sunday without fail and I visited you less often than I should have. Dad you gave me far more than you gave your grandchildren, you gave me yourself and the knowledge that my Dad was a man, a decent man.

Keep on sailing Kid and when I come into dock, which I hope is not for a long time, keep a berth open for me."

THE END

Rugby Union is only a game

Some like it, some don't.

But to me, through the context of that game,
I experienced what at the time
were bitter disappointments and unreserved,
often undeserved, joys.
And now I know none of it really mattered.

One's just left with happy memories
of friendships and a boy scout philosophy
for which I am grateful.
Which is:-

That there's no mileage in bad mouthing anyone,
it just demeans you.
If something is important to you, you pick
yourself up and fight.
However, when and if things bounce your way,
don't be beholden to anyone,
enjoy them, run them for everything,
'cos as the man said
"Kid, you're a long time dead".

What amazes me is I never made it big in the boy scouts.